PRESENTED TO:

FROM:

DATE:

"I WILL SEEK YOUR FACE: 31 DAYS OF KNOWING GOD BY NAME"

Callan —

May you come to Know
the Source of Divine Life in
ever increasing ways!

In His Love,
Carmen [signature]
II Cor 13:14

I WILL SEEK YOUR FACE:
31 DAYS OF KNOWING GOD BY NAME

BY REV. CONNIE SCOTT

Touching lives through Worship and the Word!

I Will Seek Your Face: 31 Days of Knowing God by Name

By Rev. Connie V. Scott

Copyright © 2011 Constant Hope Publishing | Voice of Hope Ministries, Inc

ISBN 10:   0-615-46850-0
ISBN 13: 978-0-615-46850-1

Constant Hope Publishing is a division of:
Voice of Hope Ministries, Inc.
P.O. Box 2344, Evanston, Wyoming 82931

307-679-2616
www.vohministries.org

Cover Design:
Connie V. Scott

Photography:
Wendy Jepsen

Cover Art:
"Casting Down Their Golden Crowns"
By Wendy Francisco © 2004
All rights reserved. Used by permission.

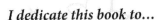

I dedicate this book to...

The Cool Chicks (you know who you are),
You encourage and inspire me.
I consider it an honor to call you friends!

Anton & Jeannie Black
For your trust, friendship, and love -
You are such amazing people,
And true spiritual parents!

ENDORSEMENTS

While reading through Connie's amazing book, I was reminded of the encounter Moses experienced, as YHWH passed before him declaring His name, to demonstrate His goodness to the people. I pray that as you devote time and attention to the Holy Spirit's guidance through these pages, that God would cause His goodness to pass before you and the presence, authority, compassion, and power of God in His name would fascinate your attention and your affections. I highly recommend Connie's work and believe in the calling and anointing of intimacy on her life as a student of worship and adoration.

~ Tommy Green, Lead Vocalist Sleeping Giant,
   Director of Revolution Reality Ministries (www.revolutionreality.org)

"This is a small book which will help you to do just what the title suggests, by simply looking at one name of God each day. Through His names, more and more of His character unfolds, and the effect is cumulative. With each passing day, God gets bigger and more amazing, each name building on and adding to the name before it until you are faced with a majesty you can barely comprehend. Knowing God by Name, by Rev. Connie Scott, is refreshing, clarifying, and beautifully written."

~ Wendy Francisco, Artist, Author, and Musician
   (www.wendyfrancisco.com)

As you read this daily devotional book, you will find yourself discovering so much more about Connie and who she is in love with. The carefully placed thoughts will stir your heart to want to wait in His presence and press into more of what Jesus wants to say to you personally in that moment. The personal way Connie has laid these thoughts out for us to enjoy is a delight. This book will energize you in a fresh way to make devotions a major ingredient in your own personal spiritual development. I have the privilege of knowing Connie, and this book brings to light again who she really is.

~ Robert Guiller, Lead Pastor of Crossroads Christian Fellowship
   (www.ccfutah.org)

"What I believe about God is the most important thing about me," said A. W. Tozer. This easy-to-read book by Connie Scott will revolutionize what you believe about God and will help you worship Him in Spirit and in Truth. Moses asked God to see His glory and God proclaimed His Name to him. His Name was revealing His nature and character. As we meditate on the names of God, we can also behold the beauty of the Lord and see His glory!

~ **Kari Browning, New Renaissance Church, Coeur d'Alene, Idaho**
   (**www.newrenaissance.us**)

Connie Scott has captured the desire of God to make Himself known to us! By looking into each name of the Lord, we can expectantly call upon each virtue in faith filled expectation. Jesus summed up His entire ministry by declaring "Father I have manifested your name..." (John 17:6). Even so, as we become familiar with who God is, in like manner, we can make Him Known.

~ **Randy DeMain, Kingdom Revelations Ministries**
   (**www.kingdomrevelation.org**)

This irresistible little devotional book is like an invitation within an invitation. From the very first day, Connie invites us to take a compelling glimpse into the meanings of some of the names our fascinating God has given Himself. But if a name is an invitation into knowledge of the one carrying the name, then the God who transcends human understanding, in His kindness towards us, has freely unveiled His very heart by revealing His Name in many facets, to us. Just as Jacob wrestled with God, asked Him for His name, and was given a blessing, we are invited through the pages of this book to enter into a dialogue with our Creator, the Lover of our souls, the self-existent One who is longing to unfold the mysteries of His identity to us...and pour out His blessing. Connie's engaging writing style flows from a worshiper's heart to create a beautiful offering of wonder and awe.

~ **Wendy Jepsen, Desert Song Ministries**
   (**www.desertsongministries.org**)

ACKNOWLEDGEMENTS

Without the encouragement, prayers and support of the following people, I could not have done this. My heartfelt thanks go out to each of you. May God bless you, as much as you have blessed me!

GOD, You are everything to me! The very breath that I breathe and the life that sustains me, is from You. What more can I give than my life in return. You are my Elohiym, Mashiach, and Ruach Adonai. I love You, Lord – Father, Son, and Holy Spirit!

WENDY *(ww)*: Thank you for pushing me to write and get this book done; for being as excited to learn and read about the nature of Elohiym, as I was to write about it; once again for taking the time to read, reread, and edit this book; and for your unmatched encouragement and support. You have not only been a vital part in the writing of this book, but your friendship and ministry has spoken volumes into my life! Love ya, sis – *cb*

WENDY FRANCISCO: For sharing your beautiful artwork and graciously allowing me to use it in the book, I thank you! *"The depth of our ministry is up to us, but the breadth is up to the Father."* You make His heart sing.

LESA *(cece)*: God is the giver of good gifts and I am thankful for the friend He has given to me. Thank you for all the prayer support, interesting conversation while watching TV and working on our laptops, and a place to crash. You're a treasure!

MYLENE & KATHY: Thank you for your prayers, suggestions, and extra sets of eyes to proof the book. I love you both!

FAMILY, FRIENDS & MINISTRY SUPPORTERS: I couldn't do this without you – thanks and God bless you all!

INTRODUCTION

Welcome and thank you for taking the time to *"seek the face"* of God. As Christians, our number one priority in life should be our relationship with the Lord. It is amazing to know the Creator of all things desires for us to spend time with Him, so we can know His heart.

Many people know a lot about God, but not too many have intimate knowledge of Him. We are able to present facts, but don't really know the heart of our Father. *"Could I be one of those people?"* This question was at the forefront of my mind as I began to write this book. Scripture gives us tremendous insight into who God is, facts that will help us in our journey, but until we begin to know His heart, they are simply words on a page.

Over the next 31 days as you study and journal, I hope your eyes will be opened and your hearts ignited as you begin to know God through His perspective…as you begin to know Him by Name. I guarantee He will breathe life into your inner man, shake inaccurate thinking, heal deep wounds, and reveal His beautiful heart to you. You won't be disappointed and you'll never be the same!

Lastly, I hope you begin to feel God's pleasure! From the very beginning of time, God has desired a love relationship. That is why we were created, yet He has given us free will to choose Him. As you spend time getting to know God, understand that you are choosing to love Him in return. It will bring joy to His heart, a smile to His face, and cause Him to pour out His love upon you! Enjoy the journey!

In His Love,
Rev. Connie V. Scott

DAY 1

ELOHIYM
אלהים

"THE ALMIGHTY ONE"

"In the beginning God created the heavens and the earth."
Genesis 1:1

From the very beginning, we see God, Elohiym revealing His character to His people. Elohiym is the first name of God in scripture and used over 2,300 times throughout the Old Testament. We do not have such a word in our own language, but in Hebrew it is a singular-plural word.

The very first glimpse God reveals is a mystery in and of itself. It is this mystery we will be searching out for all eternity. Elohiym, the Almighty One, the Almighty God, refers to the plurality of our One God. He reveals the fullness of the Godhead with a single word. He not only expresses His power and strength, but His desire for relationship with those He has created... you.

Today, allow Elohiym; Father, Son, and Holy Spirit to unveil new revelation of Himself to your heart. Our mysterious God wants nothing more than to be known by us all.

PRAYER: Father, as I embark on this journey of knowing You through Your names, please open the eyes of my heart to receive all that You desire to impart into my life. Let today be the first of many days that I see a new facet of who You are. In Jesus' Name, Amen.

DAY 2

ELOHAY KEDEM
אלהים קדם

"GOD OF THE BEGINNING"

"The eternal God is your refuge, and underneath are the everlasting arms..." Deuteronomy 33:27a

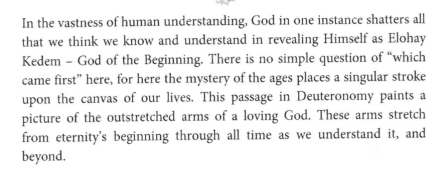

In the vastness of human understanding, God in one instance shatters all that we think we know and understand in revealing Himself as Elohay Kedem – God of the Beginning. There is no simple question of "which came first" here, for here the mystery of the ages places a singular stroke upon the canvas of our lives. This passage in Deuteronomy paints a picture of the outstretched arms of a loving God. These arms stretch from eternity's beginning through all time as we understand it, and beyond.

This is not a mere man whose beginning is marked on the calendar, for He encompasses all things. Elohay Kedem is the uncreated One. He is the One who holds all time in the very palm of His hand. Before time itself, before creation, before all things He was and He is!

Words fall short in expressing Elohay Kedem, and our human understanding cannot fathom the enormity of Him, but it should bring us great comfort in knowing there is One who has seen it all. Our amazing God of the Beginning has stretched through eternity to meet you.

PRAYER: Father, I can hardly begin to understand the complexity of who You are and yet You have reached through all time and space to meet me. My heart overflows with thanksgiving to think of the great love You must have for mankind. As I come to understand You as the God of the Beginning, help me to build my life upon You as the very foundation of all things. In Jesus' Name, Amen.

DAY 3

ABBA
Αββα

"FATHER"

"For you did not receive the spirit of bondage again to fear, but you received the Spirit of adoption by whom we cry out, "Abba, Father."
Romans 8:15

Close your eyes for a few moments and think back to your childhood and the relationship you had with your father. When I think back to my childhood, I have fond memories of spending time with my dad. I recall playing football in the front yard of our house in California. I remember the two story playhouse he built us, because there were no trees in the yard. I even remember him running beside me as I was learning to ride my bike. But, the most powerful memory I have of my father was the day he jumped into my grandmother's pond fully clothed to save my life. I have amazing memories of the love my dad has shown throughout the years, but I know not everyone has had such warm memories.

Oftentimes, our earthly relationships shape our heavenly perspectives. We see God through the experiences and filters developed by the relationships we've had with our own fathers. If our interactions were healthy, then our perception of God is more positive, but if *dad* wasn't quite all he could have been, we tend to see God in a similar light. One thing I've learned about my Father in heaven is that His love for me far exceeds any love and kindness I have known from my earthly father.

By all rights, we don't deserve such goodness. However, through Jesus, we have been adopted into the family of God. He chose us and will never let us go! His love is not dependent upon our works or goodness, because His love is constant and never-ending. There is nothing you or I can do to make Him love us any more than He does today. Regardless of our earthly relationships, we can know God as Abba – Daddy or Papa God. Abba wants us to know Him intimately. His desire is for us to cry out to Him when we fall down, and jump on His lap and tell Him our secrets. Papa wants to play hide and seek with us and He'll even let us win from time to time. He'll protect, guide, and comfort us. He'll sing over us, rejoice with us. Abba is the best Dad we could ever have, and He calls us His own.

PRAYER: Abba, today I am truly thankful I've been adopted into Your family. You've chosen me and I choose You. No matter how my relationship was and is with my earthly father, I ask You to show me a right view of You as my Daddy, my Abba. Where there are *father wounds* in my life, I ask You to heal my heart and bring restoration to my life. In Jesus' Name, Amen.

DAY 4

ELOHAY KEDOSHIM
אלהים קדוש
EL HAKADOSH
אל קדוש

"THE HOLY GOD"

"Speak to all the congregation of the children of Israel, and say to them: 'You shall be holy, for I the LORD your God am holy."
Leviticus 19:2

"But Joshua said to the people, "You cannot serve the LORD, for He is a holy God. He is a jealous God; He will not forgive your transgressions nor your sins." Joshua 24:19

"But the LORD of hosts shall be exalted in judgment, and God who is holy shall be hallowed in righteousness." Isaiah 5:16

It has been said that God cannot be in the presence of sin, but this is an incorrect approach to the holiness of God. God is not intimidated by sin. He is not afraid of the wickedness of mankind, nor is He fearful of the evil that is so evident in our world today. When we approach the holiness of God, it isn't a matter of Him being able to bear it, but rather evil cannot bear the weight, the glory, and the purity of God's holiness. In the presence of Elohay Kedoshim or El HaKadosh is the purest of existence for there is no darkness, no selfishness, and no hint of anything that is contrary to holiness.

In the passages of scripture above, there is heaviness to God's holiness. In Leviticus, the children of Israel were commanded to live holy, because El HaKodosh is holy. Joshua proclaimed to the people, "They cannot serve the LORD, for He is a holy God." In Isaiah, they were (as are we) exhorted to exalt and hallow God, because He is holy and righteous. It was impossible for man to walk in complete holiness under the law, and without Christ, even our best efforts fall utterly short of measuring to the holiness of Elohay Kedoshim.

Should we watch certain movies? Is it right to speak a certain way? Are we permitted to go into certain businesses and establishments? What is the appropriate type of clothing for a person to wear? The questions could go on and on. Religion will always have a list of "dos & don'ts", but when we live our lives for our Holy God, then we must simply ask one question… Is my lifestyle, the things I do, the company I keep, the places I go, my speech, etc. – will these things of my life survive the presence of pure holiness?

Today, allow the weight of God's holiness to rest upon you. May it be a consuming fire of purification (Hebrew 12:29) and a comforting blanket of hope, knowing we are being transformed into His image (II Corinthians 3:18) through Jesus. Let it be a burden we all carry with us into every situation, every relationship, and every endeavor until we have greater revelation of our God, who is holy.

PRAYER: Father, where I fall short in understanding You as a holy God, please bring wisdom and understanding to my life. I realize You can be anywhere, but my life may not be able to remain in Your presence. I want to know You as Elohay Kedoshim, the Holy God, so I may serve and live holy as You are holy. Teach me the reality of Your holiness today. In Jesus' Name, Amen.

DAY 5

YHVH M'KADESH
יהוה קדש

"THE LORD WHO MAKES HOLY"

"The nations also will know that I, the LORD, sanctify Israel, when My sanctuary is in their midst forevermore." Ezekiel 37:28

"Speak also to the children of Israel, saying: 'Surely My Sabbaths you shall keep, for it is a sign between Me and you throughout your generations, that you may know that I am the LORD who sanctifies you." Exodus 31:13

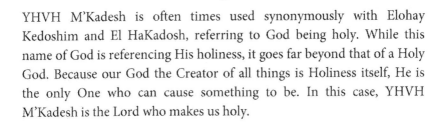

YHVH M'Kadesh is often times used synonymously with Elohay Kedoshim and El HaKadosh, referring to God being holy. While this name of God is referencing His holiness, it goes far beyond that of a Holy God. Because our God the Creator of all things is Holiness itself, He is the only One who can cause something to be. In this case, YHVH M'Kadesh is the Lord who makes us holy.

What a beautiful aspect of God's heart is revealed through this name. He commands us to be holy as He is holy (Leviticus. 19:2), but is also the means by which we live out this holiness. He desires to give us everything we need to live, so we can live in constant communion with Him.

Sin is striving for something that is already ours in God. Adam and Eve had everything they needed in the garden, but were told not to eat of the tree of knowledge of good and evil. They didn't need to eat of its fruit because they had communion with the Creator of the tree itself! As they walked with God daily, He revealed His wisdom, His purposes, and His heart to them. When we fail to realize that we have all we need in God, we will strive to be like Him, yet fail miserably.

We are reminded in the passages above that it is God who sanctifies His people as they commune with Him; making their hearts a habitation of His presence – a sanctuary for Him to dwell in. We are also reminded of the Sabbaths. These are days of rest and reflection on YHVH M'Kadesh.

In the business of life, slow down. Stop the striving and rest in the arms of a Holy God, who makes us holy as we fellowship with Him.

PRAYER: Father, help me not get caught up in the hustle and bustle of the world today, but let me rest in knowing all I need is in You. When I begin to strive to be holy, remind me that You are the source of life and holiness, and, as I gaze upon You, I will become more like you. Father God, thank You for making me holy. In Jesus' Name, Amen.

DAY 6

YHVH
יהוה

"LORD"

*"And God said to Moses, "I AM WHO I AM." And He said,
"Thus you shall say to the children of Israel, 'I AM has sent me to
you.'" Moreover God said to Moses, "Thus you shall say to the
children of Israel: 'The LORD God of your fathers, the God of
Abraham, the God of Isaac, and the God of Jacob, has sent
me to you. This is My name forever, and this is My
memorial to all generations.'" Exodus 3:14-15*

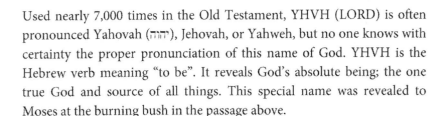

Used nearly 7,000 times in the Old Testament, YHVH (LORD) is often pronounced Yahovah (יהוה), Jehovah, or Yahweh, but no one knows with certainty the proper pronunciation of this name of God. YHVH is the Hebrew verb meaning "to be". It reveals God's absolute being; the one true God and source of all things. This special name was revealed to Moses at the burning bush in the passage above.

Yahweh is the existent One – Who is, Who was, and Who always will be. In this name, God does not simply disclose one element of His character, but proclaims, "This is My eternal name; the name that will be known throughout all generations. I AM WHO I AM!" This name encapsulates all of the names God has made known to humanity.

In the natural, we have layers of information locked away within us, and not all people are allowed to know the deepest most intimate facts of our lives. Depending on our relationship with an individual, this will be the basis for which we determine what information is made known. Those we are closest to, tend to know the most about us. Because this is how we live out our lives here on earth, we assume God is the same way. However, He is not bound by our way of thinking.

Be encouraged today! YHVH, the LORD Jehovah, the existent One has revealed and continues to disclose the most intimate facets of His being. He isn't waiting for you to be His closest companion, but chooses to unveil all of who He is in the hopes of drawing you closer to Him. He lays it all out on the line and says, "This is who I AM."

PRAYER: Father God, my mind can hardly begin to understand the enormity of who You are, and yet You freely continue to reveal Yourself to me. I am so thankful that You love me so much to continue to make Yourself known, even when I don't understand. Please help me understand and know You as LORD, the One who is, and who is all things. In Jesus' Name, Amen.

DAY 7

ELOHIYM CHAIYIM
אלהים חי

"THE LIVING GOD"

"But the LORD is the true God, he is the living God, and an everlasting king: at his wrath the earth shall tremble, and the nations shall not be able to abide his indignation." Jeremiah 10:10

The one thing that separates Christianity from all other religions and belief systems is the fact that we serve a living God – Elohiym Chaiyim. Derived from the Hebrew root word Chayah, which means to live, to have life, to continue in life, remain alive, to sustain life, to live on or upon, to live prosperously, and to revive – there is no doubt, our God is Alive! Not only is He the beginning of all things, He is the end of all things. He is the Alpha & Omega. In Him is life and that life is never ending, because He is the everlasting, living God.

There are many religious leaders who walked the earth and died. They were buried and when you visit their tombs, they are still in them. However, the tomb of Christ is empty, for He is not there. As scripture proclaims, "He has risen!" Even the written Word of God is living! The author of Hebrews said, *"For the word of God is living and powerful, and sharper than any two-edged sword, piercing even to the division of soul and spirit, and of joints and marrow, and is a discerner of the thoughts and intents of the heart"* (Hebrews 4:12).

Knowing that we have a living God should bring great joy and peace that is truly supernatural. Because our God is alive, He has not left humanity alone, nor is He a distant dead God who is unable to hear us. Someone who is dead cannot bring life. Someone who is dead cannot speak life into situations. Someone who is dead cannot sustain life in others. Someone who is dead is dead, but where there is life...there is hope! There is hope for new things to be birthed in us and through us. There is hope that our Elohiym Chaiyim will breathe life on the embers of our lives and revive us. There is hope because He is alive!

Today, I encourage you to look at the things in your life that appear to be dead or barely hanging on to life. Are those things under the Lordship of God? If not, take those things and lay them before Elohiym Chaiyim, the living God, and allow Him to revive, restore, and renew. Perhaps some of them need to be buried, while others should be alive and thriving. Regardless, let God make the final decision. If we willingly place all things in His hands, He is the One who can and will bring eternal, supernatural life to us, because He is life itself.

PRAYER: Living God, I admit there are areas in my life that seem dead or nearly so. I lay them at Your feet today. Remove those things in my life that should not remain, and breathe Your sustaining life upon those things You want in my life. Father, I pray for greater revelation of what it means to serve and have relationship with Elohiym Chaiyim, the living God. In Jesus' Name, Amen.

DAY 8

EL ELYON
אל עללי

"THE MOST HIGH GOD"

"Then Nebuchadnezzar went near the mouth of the burning fiery furnace and spoke, saying, "Shadrach, Meshach, and Abed-Nego, servants of the Most High God, come out, and come here." Then Shadrach, Meshach, and Abed-Nego came from the midst of the fire." Daniel 3:26

Throughout the earth today, many face death for choosing to serve another god other than the god of their land. Strangely enough, their suffering is quite similar to what Shadrach, Meshach, and Abed-Nego faced in the book of Daniel.

Nebuchadnezzar was the king of Babylon, who sent out the decree that all inhabitants of his lands were to worship him alone. Those who did not follow the command were to be burned for their disobedience. What separated these three young men was Who they served. They followed the God of Abraham, Isaac, and Jacob – El Elyon, the Most High God. Determined not to dishonor God, they disobeyed the edict of the land and refused to bow and worship the king, but instead worshiped the King of kings! Knowing death would come to them if they were caught; these three still chose to worship the only true God. Scripture tells us they knew God would deliver them from Nebuchadnezzar's hands, and if by chance He didn't, they would rather die serving Yahweh than to live denying Him.

Today, we see a similar scenario taking place all over the world. People fear for their lives for choosing Christ over another, and some are too afraid to give their lives to Jesus. Even some Christians walk in fear, not for their physical lives, but in fear of being rejected by others, so they do not disclose their true identity. Perhaps we need a greater revelation of El Elyon – the Most High God!

Most of us will never face the *fire* while serving Jesus, but ask this question: "What would I do if my life were on the line for God?" Would you cower down to the authorities of the land and deny your God? Would you secretly serve Him, so as not to be caught? Or, would you, like the three young men, openly pray to El Elyon? Maybe your *fire* is the rejection of family and friends – maybe it is your life on the line. Regardless, just as Shadrach, Meshach, and Abed-Nego were saved from death, El Elyon will deliver you. He is greater than any circumstance and more powerful than any foe.

No matter the situation, call upon God today. Trust that He will and is able to lift you out of any *fire*. As a matter of fact, He will be the fourth man in the furnace, and when you come out, you won't even have the smell of smoke on you, but you will have a new song in your mouth (Psalm 40). It was the unwavering commitment to serve El Elyon that changed Nebuchadnezzar. He acknowledged El Elyon, the Most High God. In a world where there are millions of gods to choose from, choose the only One who stands alone – He is the Most High God – El Elyon!

PRAYER: Father, I admit at times I walk in the fear of man and hide my identity, but I long to walk in greater boldness. Today, I ask You to reveal Yourself to me as El Elyon, the Most High God. Help me understand what Shadrach, Meshach, and Abed-Nego knew. I give You permission to transform and refine me in all areas of life, because I believe there is no One greater than You. In Jesus' Name, Amen.

DAY 9

YHVH KANNA
יהוה קנא

"THE JEALOUS GOD"

"...For you shall worship no other god, for the LORD, whose name is Jealous, is a jealous God." Exodus 34:14

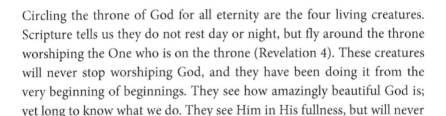

Circling the throne of God for all eternity are the four living creatures. Scripture tells us they do not rest day or night, but fly around the throne worshiping the One who is on the throne (Revelation 4). These creatures will never stop worshiping God, and they have been doing it from the very beginning of beginnings. They see how amazingly beautiful God is; yet long to know what we do. They see Him in His fullness, but will never experience intimate relationship with Him like we can.

We are often told God needs our worship, but this is not true. He has worship. All of heaven worships Him. Every angel that He created serves and worships Him. Our God longs for relationship with humanity. He fashioned us in His very image and breathed the breath of life into us, so we could commune with Him. Oh, the joy in His heart as He walked with Adam in the cool of the day (Genesis 3:8). Can you imagine the sorrow He must have felt when Adam and Eve ate the fruit? From that point forward, He was trying to commune with His people and yet, they continued to push Him away.

Did you know God has emotions? In today's passage, God reveals the magnitude of His love. YHVH Kanna tells us to love no one else, because He loves us beyond human comprehension. It is a warning not given in anger, but wholehearted passionate love. If we read between the lines, He is saying, "Don't go looking for love in other places. Other lovers will disappoint you. Other lovers will leave you. Other lovers will hurt you!" God does not need our worship. YHVH Kanna longs for our love, needs our love, and is jealous for our love!

PRAYER: Father, I love You, and yet I really don't know love. Your Word says that You are the Lover of my soul, and long for me to know Love that is beyond understanding. I ask You to help me know the depths of Your desire for me, my YHVH Kanna. In Jesus' Name, Amen.

ᗞAY 10

ᗐSH OKHLAH
אש אכל

"ᕦONSUMING ᕦIRE"

"For the LORD your God is a consuming fire, a jealous God."
Deuteronomy 4:24

"Therefore, since we are receiving a kingdom which cannot be shaken, let us have grace, by which we may serve God acceptably with reverence and godly fear. For our God is a consuming fire."
Hebrews 12:29

Is there anything better than a campfire? It brings warmth on a cool night in the mountains, and allows us to make the tastiest of S'mores. Fire left uncontained will overtake and destroy everything in its path though. Every year, we read of fires that are out of control. Thousands of acres of land are consumed, homes threatened, and lives forever changed because of one small spark.

Throughout scripture we see fire. It is used in the ceremonial sacrifices (II Chronicles 7:1), in judgment of wickedness (Leviticus 9:24), and in vindication of the righteous (I Kings 18:30-39). In its first reference in Genesis 15, we see fire referring to the very presence of God. More than just a representation, God is fire – Esh okhlah – Consuming fire. He was a cloud by day and fire by night (Exodus 13:21) while the children of Israel wandered in the desert. He sits as a refiner's fire (Malachi 3:2)

49

burning away the impurities in our lives. Esh okhlah, our God who is a Consuming Fire is uncontrollable and if we attempt to control Him, we will get burned.

Esh okhlah desired to commune with His people in the desert, but they sent Moses to speak to Him instead. They feared God because of the fire. However, Moses was drawn to the flame and found favor. Scripture tells us God spoke with Moses like a friend (Exodus 33:11) and revealed His ways to him (Psalm 103:7). God is calling us to know His heart and His ways today. He longs to speak with us face to face, for us to look into His eyes of passionate fiery love (Revelation 1:14), and give Him permission to be Esh okhlah, our Consuming Fire. All things will be consumed by His flame and what remains will be pure gold.

PRAYER: Father, I thank You for Your fire. It is the fire of passion that draws me to You. It is the fire that consumes everything that is not of You. Even though at times the fire hurts, I give You permission to refine me, because I know that You sit carefully watching and will not allow me to be harmed. You are Esh okhlah, the Consuming Fire. Help me to have a greater understanding of this facet of who You are. In Jesus' Name, Amen.

DAY 11

ELOHAY TEHILATI
אלהים תהללה

"GOD OF MY PRAISE"

To the Chief Musician. A Psalm of David.
"Do not keep silent, O God of My praise!" Psalm 109:1

How befitting this passage of scripture is, as we continue to know God by name. In it, we hear the cry of King David's heart toward his God, who is not only worthy of all praise, but is praise itself. In a time when David's enemies were rising up against him, he lifted his voice to Elohay Tehilati. And, this was no simple song!

Tehilati comes from the Hebrew word Tehillah, which refers to the spontaneous song of the Sprit, or *new song*. This song is not rehearsed and has never been sung before the ears of man, but erupts from the very core of who we are. The Hebrew root word for Tehillah is Halal, which is the unhindered, undignified, boastful, crazy praise to God. In Psalm 40:3, the psalmist says, *"He has put a new song in my mouth – Praise to our God; many will see it and fear, and will trust in the Lord."* God Himself has put this new song in us. He is the song, and His song has no barriers. He is the praise!

As we begin to understand Elohay Tehilati; the God of My Praise, we will begin to see how important our worship is. This very worship is what God inhabits in Psalm 22:3, and is a powerful weapon against the enemy.

Today, let your cry be, "O God of my praise, do not keep silent. Let Your voice ever be heard in my life; and let Your praise ever be on my lips!"

PRAYER: Father, I give You all praise and glory today! May I ever be mindful that You are the very source of my praise. No circumstance, no possession, and no person can create praise in my spirit – You are the only worthy One. I pray for insight into the power and purpose of my praise on the earth. Help me be unhindered in my expression of praise to You. Open my heart to truly know that I will know You better, as I begin to understand You as my praise. In Jesus' Name, Amen.

DAY 12

EL ROʾI
אל ראי

"THE GOD WHO SEES"

*"Then she called the name of the LORD who spoke to her,
You-Are-the-God-Who-Sees; for she said, 'Have I also
here seen Him who sees me?'" Genesis 16:13*

All too often, a veil is placed over our minds, hindering our perceptions of God. Our environment, childhood memories, culture, and spiritual backgrounds tint the lenses through which we see the world and the Lord. These lenses are further colored by our experiences with those who act and/or speak in the Name of the Lord.

Instead of seeing the purity of the Creator of All, we see a tyrannical dictator who has handed down the list of "dos and don'ts"; making life difficult and waiting for us to make one wrong move so He can punish us. Or, we see Him as an unhappy angry God with whom we must appease with *right* living so as not to make Him angrier. With this perception, we may begin to walk in fear and keep El Roʾi at a distance.

As challenging as it may be, I exhort you to remove the glasses and allow our loving, joyful God to shatter the wrong thinking and misguided perceptions. Hagar (Ishmael's mother) had reason to have incorrect thoughts of this God whom Abraham served. Perhaps, like so many of us, she thought His eyes were ever on her waiting to strike. Or, she felt invisible altogether; believing this God would have nothing to do with her since she was sent away by Abraham. But, El Ro'i, the God who sees us is not planning His attack. He is watching over His creation and His children to keep them from harm. Ishmael and his mother were perishing in the desert, but His eyes were on them the entire time, and when she cried out to Him, He rescued them because He is the God who sees.

We have a wonderful God who hears our petitions (Psalm 40), because He is attentive to our voice. We have an amazing Lord whose eyes search to and fro, longing to find hearts that are sincere and friendly toward Him (II Chronicles 16:9). We have a loving Father, who doesn't want us to be afraid of Him, but to reverence and have awe for Him, all the while knowing that we are ever in His hands, His heart, and His sight.

PRAYER: Father, I am so thankful for Your loving-kindness. Where my perceptions of You are incorrect, I pray that You will reveal the truth to me. I give You permission to shatter the tinted lenses that color my perspective of You. You are El Ro'i, the God who sees me. Yes, you see my every move and know every motive of my heart, but You see me through the blood of Jesus. You see me at the point of my need and because You see, I know You will always be there for me. Where I struggle to believe this, help my unbelief...help me see You for who You really are.

DAY 13

YHWH YIR'EH
יהוה ירה

"THE LORD WHO SEES AND PROVIDES"

"Then Abraham lifted his eyes and looked, and there behind him was a ram caught in a thicket by its horns. So Abraham went and took the ram, and offered it up for a burnt offering instead of his son. And Abraham called the name of the place, The-LORD-Will-Provide; as it is said to this day, 'In the Mount of the LORD it shall be provided'." Genesis 22:13-14

YHWH Yireh is the compound name of God, given by Abraham to venerate the covenant-keeping grace God had shown him on Mount Moriah. At face value, this is a beautiful story of Abraham's obedience to the Lord, and Yahweh's goodness to provide a sacrifice in place of Isaac. However, in order to really understand YHWH Yireh, we must go beyond the surface; diving deep into the heart of God.

While we understand the meaning of YHWH Yireh to be "The Lord Who Provides", Yireh is actually derived from the Hebrew word Ra'ah, which means to see, to perceive, to discern, and to foresee. This sheds amazing light on God's character. YHWH, the existent One, not only sees, but foresees all of our needs, all of our desires. The uncreated One, who holds time in His hands sees all the days of your life and knows your need.

Dig yet deeper and you will begin to understand the true heart of the Father revealed in this name. Moriah, the place where God told Abraham to sacrifice Isaac means "chosen by Jehovah". This mountain on the eastern edge of Jerusalem was the location of Solomon's temple. The root word for Moriah is actually Ra'ah, the same as Yireh – our God foresees, and provides!

YHWH Yireh provided the ram for Abraham's sacrifice saving Isaac's life. YHWH Yireh provided Solomon's temple so the children of Israel would have a place to worship and sacrifice, in essence, saving their lives. YHWH Yireh saw and provided Jesus, the ultimate sacrifice, meeting the needs of all humanity. Is there anything too great for our God?

Be encouraged today, as you lean into and call upon YHWH Yireh, the Lord Who Sees and Provides. He knew your need before you even realized you had one!

PRAYER: Father, I am overwhelmed by Your goodness today. You are YHWH Yireh, the God who sees all the days of my life and has provision enough for every day, every situation, every need – spirit, soul, and body. I thank You for the greatest sacrifice of all – Jesus. You didn't give Your only Son because I was obedient; You gave because of Your great love. Continue to reveal Yourself to me as YHWH Yireh, because today I have a glimpse into Your heart. In Jesus' Name, Amen.

DAY 14

EL HANE'EMAN
אל אמן

"THE FAITHFUL GOD"

*"Therefore know that the LORD your God, He is God,
the faithful God who keeps covenant and mercy for a
thousand generations with those who love Him and
keep His commandments." Deuteronomy 7:9*

Located in Dubai, Burj Khalifa is the world's tallest structure reaching some 2,717 feet into the air.[1] This building is taller than any man-made structure ever built. It is fair to say that the builders made sure this building was structurally sound, and various tests were done throughout the construction to ensure its safety. If you were a tenant of this building, you would make sure that it had been built to code. No matter what floor you were on, you would want to feel safe and secure knowing your building was firm, reliable, and made to last, upholding all of the weight set upon it, right?

El HaNe'eman, our faithful God is bigger still. Derived from the Hebrew root word 'Aman (אמן), which means steady, firm, to support, trust, to be established, uphold, nourish, foster, and to be a pillar, El HaNe'eman is the foundation of all existence and because He holds us, we have nothing to worry about. He is secure, true, and faithful. Throughout history, God has established covenant with many people. He made a covenant with Moses and delivered the children of Israel out of Egyptian bondage. He made a covenant with Abraham, promising him that he would be the father of many nations (Genesis 17), and it came to pass. However, the greatest of all covenants was and is salvation through Jesus Christ. We often think this covenant was set in motion when Adam and Eve sinned, but scripture tells us that He was the Lamb slain before the foundations of the world (Revelation 13:8).

We have such a beautiful promise in today's scripture – El HaNe'eman, our faithful God keeps His promises to a thousand generations. A biblical generation is typically thought to be 40 years, so 1,000 generations is equal to 40,000 years. His faithfulness lasts well beyond our natural lives. His faithfulness will never run short. He has been faithful to every generation, and we will not be left wanting. *"Unless the LORD builds the house, they labor in vain who build it"* (Psalm 127:1). At the end of the age, Burj Khalifa will not stand. It is a structure made by man. However, El HaNe'eman is sure. When we build our lives upon Him, we have nothing to worry about, because He is Faithful.

PRAYER: Father, today I choose to step into covenant with You, El HaNe'eman. You are faithful and true, and I completely trust You. I thank You for Your faithfulness throughout eternity; knowing the covenants You make will never end. Continue to reveal to me Your faithfulness in every area of my life. In Jesus Name, Amen.

DAY 15

YHVH SHALOM
יהוה שלום

"THE LORD IS PEACE"

*"Then the LORD said to him, "Peace be with you; do not fear, you
shall not die." So Gideon built an altar there to the LORD,
and called it The-LORD-Is-Peace. To this day it is still in
Ophrah of the Abiezrites." Judges 6:23-24*

We should not be surprised with what is happening in our world today.
Scripture plainly tells us of what is to come in the last days. Luke 21:10-11
says, *"Then He said to them, 'Nation will rise against nation, and kingdom
against kingdom. And there will be great earthquakes in various places,
and famines and pestilences; and there will be fearful sights and great signs
from heaven...'"* Even in today's passage, we see Gideon living in a time
of war. He was hiding in fear, but YHVH Shalom came and spoke a word
of peace to Him.

Peace doesn't automatically mean the lack of turmoil. In this life we will
have challenges and difficulties, but we also have a God who is with us,
speaking peace over the situation (John 16:33). My question for you
today is, "Are you positioned to receive the peace?" YHVH, our Existent
One, the I Am that I Am is here for you today and His desire is to be
Shalom – Peace in the midst of all your circumstances.

Shalom means completeness, soundness, welfare, safety, health, prosperity, quiet, tranquility, contentment, and friendship with man and God, especially in covenant relationship. It truly is the picture of nothing being missing or broken in respect to your life. You may ask if such peace is attainable. The answer is very simply, "Yes!" However, there is a small condition… If we attempt to gain this peace in our own strength, using our own abilities, then we will never walk in the Shalom of God. He is Peace, so all we must do is lean into Him, lay our lives at His feet, and trust in Him.

Gideon understood who his God was. He realized his God was the source of peace. So much so, that he built an altar and called it YHVH Shalom. Like Gideon, we build altars, but too often they are altars of fear, worry, doubt, and unbelief. We focus on all that is happening around us, which causes sickness and brokenness, instead of placing our focus on the Lord. What things in your life today have missing parts or are seemingly broken? Where is there discontentment? Are you longing for tranquility and a quieting in your life: spirit, soul or body? Today, allow YHVH Shalom to speak peace over, in, and through your life. Let the Peace Speaker speak peace in such a way that it surrounds you like a warm blanket. As you do this, you will realize there is nothing missing and nothing broken in your life.

PRAYER: Father, so often I have inner turmoil that brings unbalance to my life and when I look at our world today, things seem so dark. Help me to lean into Your strength and peace today. Help me walk in greater revelation of YHVH Shalom, the God of my peace; the One who mends the broken places, keeps me safely in His grasp, brings favor and contentment, and completes me. I acknowledge today that You are the only one who can do this in my life. Have Your perfect way in me today. In Jesus' Name, Amen.

DAY 16

ADONAI TZURI
אדון צור

"GOD OF MY STRENGTH... GOD MY ROCK"

"The LORD lives! Blessed be my Rock! Let God be exalted, the Rock of my salvation!" 2 Samuel 22:47

"As it is written: 'Behold, I lay in Zion a stumbling stone and rock of offense, and whoever believes on Him will not be put to shame.'" Romans 9:33

In 1834, Edward Mote penned these familiar words... *"On Christ the solid rock I stand. All other ground is sinking sand. All other ground is sinking sand."*[2] Each day that passes brings us that much closer to the return of Jesus Christ. The Bible tells us that peoples' hearts will grow cold and the days will become increasingly evil as we see that final day approaching. It doesn't take too long to realize the shaking that our world is going through. Natural disasters are becoming more common, and our economy is questionable. If we take our eyes off of God in the hard times, the shaking will overtake us!

When the world all around shakes, it is so important to grab hold of the only One who is immovable and unshakable... Adonai Tzuri – the God who is our strength and our rock! Tzuri or Petra ($\pi\epsilon\tau\rho\alpha$) in Greek, paints the picture of strength and security, protection, and a fortress of stone we can run into. Christ is our Rock!

In today's passage, we see that Christ the Rock is a rock of offense to those who do not know Him, but is the Rock of Salvation for those who call Him Savior. He is the rock we build our lives upon. *"Therefore whoever hears these sayings of Mine, and does them, I will liken him to a wise man who built his house on the rock: and the rain descended, the floods came, and the winds blew and beat on that house; and it did not fall, for it was founded on the rock. But everyone who hears these sayings of Mine, and does not do them, will be like a foolish man who built his house on the sand: and the rain descended, the floods came, and the winds blew and beat on that house; and it fell. And great was its fall."* (Matthew 7:24-27).

When we study out this passage in Matthew, we learn that the wise man built his house on Adonai Tzuri, God our Rock, and when the most violent of storms came against this house, it stood. But the foolish ones built upon sand and when the slightest of winds came, it couldn't stand. Be encouraged today in knowing your God is the Rock of ages, who is unshakable in any circumstance! Take your stand upon this rock. Build your life upon this foundation. Anchor yourself in Adonai Tzuri, because He is the only One who can withstand any shaking, any wind, all circumstances – anything that might come against you!

PRAYER: Father, at times it feels like all hell is coming against me. I am so thankful that You are the cleft in the rock – my protection. But more importantly, You are the Rock I choose to build my life upon. I pray for greater revelation of Adonai Tzuri, my Master, my Rock, my all in all. In Jesus' Name, Amen.

DAY 17

JEHOVAH ROHI
יהוה רעה

"THE LORD MY SHEPHERD"

*"The LORD is my shepherd; I shall not want. He makes
me to lie down in green pastures; He leads me beside the
still waters. He restores my soul; He leads me in the paths
of righteousness for His name's sake." Psalm 23:1-3*

Are you stressed out? Does it seem like there is never enough time in
your day to get everything done? If you are like most people, you said,
"Yes, my days are packed!" Our world is a busy place. Many combine
family life with work life, and toss church life in the mix. Then, if
anything happens that shouldn't be in that mix, it freaks us out. Thank
goodness our Father God is Jehovah Rohi, the Lord our Shepherd.

King David shared the ups and downs that many of us face. He lived in a
different time, but he dealt with wars, unhappy employees, starving
people, and an array of personal issues. However, he had a revelation of
who his God was. In today's passage, we see Jehovah Rohi shepherding
David's heart. In the midst of turbulence, David handed over control and
leadership to God, and God took control and gently led him to those still
waters and green peaceful pastures.

Can you picture our loving Shepherd guiding you with His rod? Or, do
you need Jehovah Rohi to lift you upon His shoulders and carry you to

safety? Rohi, in Hebrew means to shepherd, tend, rule, teach, and feed; to associate with, be a special friend, and to be a companion. The existent One desires to feed, guide, and protect you, His friend and companion. Today, allow God to take control of the chaos in your life, and your life itself! Let Jehovah Rohi calm the waters while you rest and receive the restoration only He can give.

PRAYER: Father, today I relinquish control and lordship of my life into Your hands. Be Jehovah Rohi, the Lord my Shepherd. Guide me with Your rod, and protect me from the enemy. Reveal to me the areas in my life that I control and have not surrendered to You. I bow my heart and life to Your leadership. In Jesus' Name, Amen.

DAY 18

JEHOVAH ROPH'EKHA
יהוה רפא

"THE LORD HEALS"

"Now when they came to Marah, they could not drink the waters of Marah, for they were bitter. Therefore the name of it was called Marah. And the people complained against Moses, saying, "What shall we drink?" So he cried out to the LORD, and the LORD showed him a tree. When he cast it into the waters, the waters were made sweet. There He made a statute and an ordinance for them, and there He tested them, and said, 'If you diligently heed the voice of the LORD your God and do what is right in His sight, give ear to His commandments and keep all His statutes, I will put none of the diseases on you which I have brought on the Egyptians. For I am the LORD who heals you.'" Exodus 15:23-26

Like the bitter waters of Marah, sickness and disease leave a horrible pungent taste in our mouths. It is a cup that many are handed and many believe it is the Lord who has placed it before them. In many ways, we are like the children of Israel - we complain and blame and cry out in anger, yet it is Jehovah Roph'ekha, the Lord our Healer who still provides the answer.

A disease is anything that causes us to be ill at ease. Disease comes in many forms and can impact us – spirit, soul, and body. When Adam and

Eve partook of the fruit, they handed over dominion to the devil, and man became susceptible to this fallen world. This may be a fact of human life, but there is a greater Truth we must grasp. When Moses asked the Lord for the answer, Jehovah Roph'ekha, the Healer told him to throw a tree into the waters, making them sweet. This is an amazing foreshadowing of Christ – the One who took upon Himself every sickness and every disease. By His stripes we were healed (Isaiah 53:5 & I Peter 2:24)!

"But He was wounded for our transgressions, He was bruised for our iniquities; the chastisement for our peace was upon Him, and by His stripes we are healed" (Isaiah 53:5). Every stripe Jesus took upon Himself, the blood that poured forth, His death, and resurrection was for our healing, our wholeness. He willingly suffered in every area – spirit, soul, and body, so we could be healed. God is not the source of sickness; nor is He a God who uses illness to discipline His people. He is Jehovah Roph'ekha, the Healer – the healer of nations, the healer of hearts, the healer of our distresses, and the healer of all sickness.

Today, I exhort you to let Jehovah Roph'ekha be health to you. Throughout the pages of scripture we see the healing power of God bring restoration. Cry out to the One who drank the cup of bitterness for you. Call upon Jehovah Roph'ekha and He will answer you.

PRAYER: Admittedly, Father, I do not understand sickness and disease. I know our bodies fall prey to the enemy and this fallen world, but I do believe with all my heart You are Jehovah Roph'ekha, the Healer and complete Health. I thank You for my life and pray for a greater understanding of You as my Healer. Show me how to cooperate with You, so I can walk in wholeness and health. And, when I don't understand, give me strength to lean into You and seek Your face for answers. In Jesus' Name, Amen.

DAY 19

JEHOVAH NISSI
יהוה נ

"THE LORD IS MY BANNER"

Then the LORD said to Moses, "Write this for a memorial in the book and recount it in the hearing of Joshua, that I will utterly blot out the remembrance of Amalek from under heaven." And Moses built an altar and called its name, The-LORD-Is-My-Banner..."
Exodus 17:14-15

Imagine you are standing on a great battlefield and the enemy is coming. The king of the land gallops by encouraging all of the troops to be brave and fight hard. He reminds them of honor and lifts high the flag of the nation, arousing shouts from the warriors. The banner, a representation of all the people, their values, their beliefs is a powerful rallying point. We've seen that scene in hundreds of movies, but Jehovah Nissi is our Banner. God is our rallying point and our means of victory; the one who fights for us, His people.

God assured Moses that He would blot out his enemy Amalek, and Moses believed his God! What enemies do you have? Have you called upon Jehovah Nissi, your Banner - something lifted up, a standard, signal, and signal pole; an ensign, banner, sign, and sail? I encourage you to lift your gaze and look upon your Banner, Jesus Christ. He was lifted up and said He would draw all mankind to Himself (John 12:32). He is our rallying point. He is our victory. He fights the battles for us, when we submit our lives to His keeping.

PRAYER: Father, I am so thankful that You are Jehovah Nissi, the Lord my Banner. Time and time again, You have been my Victor, and the Standard I so desperately need. In times of peace or in looming battle, help me keep my gaze on You. In Jesus' Name, Amen.

Day 20

Adonai
אדון

"Lord"

*"A son honors his father, and a servant his master. If then I am the
Father, where is My honor? And if I am a Master, where is My
reverence? Says the LORD of hosts to you priests who despise My
name. Yet you say, 'In what way have we despised Your name?'"*
Malachi 1:6

Many years ago, I heard a song that was talking about how we address
God. In the lyric, the writer suggested calling Him *"God"*, seemed too
casual and *"Lord"* too formal. Every so often that song comes to mind as I
think about my relationship with Him. Have I set strange definitions on
the names of God? How intimate am I with Him? Is there a name that I
am uncomfortable using in reference to God, and if so, why?

Most believers are comfortable using names such as God, Savior, Lord,
Jesus, Holy Spirit, and Father. Some may dive deeper and try out names
like Abba, Papa, Friend, Lover, Jehovah, and even Yahweh. The names
we use to reference the One we love and honor is often a reflection of our
knowledge of and relationship with Him.

In the passage above, God is addressing His priests who were not
honoring Him. They were presenting offerings that were actually
displeasing. Perhaps it was because they didn't really know Him as they

thought. Maybe they understood Him as Creator and Provider, but didn't know Him as Adonai. How do you address the King of the Universe and Creator of all things? How do you honor the One who deserves all honor?

Adonai is a reference to the lordship of God. It is derived from the Hebrew root word Adown, which means superintendent of a household, husband, governor, prince, king, lord, and master. Our Adonai is the King of all kings and Lord of all lords. He is the Superintendent of heaven and earth. He is Lord and Master! Yet, He is not looking for slaves to mindlessly serve Him. He is inviting His prophets, kings, and priests – the believer to serve and honor Him. This invitation is for us to enter into a place of Indentured Servitude.

An indentured servant is a free person who willfully gives his or her life to become a servant. They lay their freedoms down to bind themselves to their master, knowing they will never have a need the master won't meet. Do you trust Adonai enough to lay down your freedoms to take up His? Do you believe His lordship will truly meet all of your needs, and guide you into all life? His rule is just. His yoke is easy. His leadership is supernatural. If you hesitate to lay down your desires, dreams, and freedoms, I encourage you to ask yourself if you really know God as Adonai, Lord and Master.

PRAYER: Father, today I acknowledge that You are Lord, You are Savior, You are King, and You are Master - Adonai in my life. Please reveal those areas in my life where I have not given lordship over to You. Show me the areas where I grasp for control, instead of allowing You to lead. I give my life to You freely, knowing You are well able to keep me in all my ways. Guide and direct me today as Adonai, my Lord and my Master. In Jesus' Name, Amen.

DAY 21

ELOHAY MISHPAT
אלהים משפט

"GOD OF JUSTICE"

"Therefore the LORD will wait, that He may be gracious to you; and therefore He will be exalted, that He may have mercy on you. For the LORD is a God of justice; blessed are all those who wait for Him."
Isaiah 30:18

In our court system, justice is represented by the balanced scales. Unfortunately, in the natural, things don't typically balance, as it is one person's perspective versus another's. Neither sees the full picture of an event and so the judge must determine where the truth lies. Often times a compromise is made and both parties go away disappointed. Or, the truth never really surfaces and the wrong person is judged and penalized. Thank goodness our God is Elohay Mishpat, the God of Justice. He sees the entire picture and knows all truth. Where humanity falls short and scales tip in unfavorable ways, the true scales of Justice (Elohay Mishpat) are always balanced.

Mishpat means justice, rightness, rectitude, seat of judgment, and litigation. It is the picture of God seated in the courtroom at the seat of judgment. He is Judge. Where many of us fear the earthly judges, our hearts should be set at ease to know that God is our Judge. He does not place the opinions or perspectives of man on His scales, nor does He simply put our faults there. Firmly sitting on one side is the truth – all of our sin, all of our motives, all of our deeds (good and bad). If that were it, then we would be condemned, but praise be to Elohay Mishpat, who places mercy, grace, and love on the other side of the scale. Tipping the scales is Jesus Himself, who covers our sins by His blood (Revelation 5:9). The cross is where judgment and mercy kissed. Jesus prevailed and true justice was handed down from the seat of judgment, the mercy seat of God!

Don't be mistaken though, as God will not allow injustice to go without punishment. Because He is Elohay Mishpat, He must see justice fulfilled. The good news is that there is One who has removed the injunction against us. Jesus became the propitiation for our sin. Now the scales are in balance, truth prevails, and we are free. Today, allow yourself to know Elohay Mishpat, for it is His justice that will cause us to cry out for mercy. It is His justice that will move us to see others set free.

PRAYER: Father, today I pray that You will open my eyes to You as Elohay Mishpat, the Judge and God of Justice. Allow me to see the scales and how they would be tipped if it weren't for Your justice. Thank You for mercy. Thank You for love. Thank You for justice. In Jesus' Name, Amen.

DAY 22

EL YESHUATI
אל ישועה

"THE GOD OF MY SALVATION"

"Behold, God is my salvation, I will trust and not be afraid;
'For YAH, the LORD, is my strength and song;
He also has become my salvation.'" Isaiah 12:2

Derived from the primitive root word Yasha (ישע) and the masculine noun Yesha (ישע), which means to save or be saved, delivered, to be liberated, to give victory to, to prosper, and to save from moral troubles. It has the same meaning as the New Testament word for salvation – Sozo (σῴζω).

Weaving its way through the pages of scripture is a scarlet thread. From Genesis to Revelation, God makes known to His people His desire to save them from all of their enemies: spiritual, physical, and mental. In times of warfare, God fought the battle for them and victory was sure. When King Saul came under great distress, God sent David to worship in his presence, ultimately driving the spirits away. He is El Yeshuati – the God of our salvation.

If we take a step back and look at the beautiful tapestry this thread has woven, we will see Jesus. El Yeshuati, not only reveals His character as a saving God to those who are in harm's way, but foretells of the Great Deliverer, the Messiah to come. Reaching through all time, He comes to save our lives from complete destruction. If we allow Him, He will knit His saving power into us through Yeshua (Jesus) and no matter what comes our way, we will have deliverance, prosperity, and salvation.

PRAYER: Father, today I ask You to be El Yeshuati, my Salvation, my Deliverer, the One who brings victory into every area of my life. I lean into you and trust that You know what is best for me. Deliver me from wrong thinking, misguided actions, and from everything that You call an enemy. In Jesus' Name, Amen.

100

DAY 23

LOGOS
Λόγος

"THE WORD"

"In the beginning was the Word, and the Word was with God, and the Word was God." John 1:1

"He was clothed with a robe dipped in blood, and His name is called The Word of God." Revelation 19:13

Before the foundations of the world were, He was. The Genesis 1:1 God, Elohyim, is the same God of John 1:1. He is Logos, the Word of God, who became flesh and dwelt among us (John 1:14). He is Jesus, the Christ; the Anointed One, who willingly gave His life (John 3:16). Logos does not simply represent the written Word of God, but is defined as being a word uttered by a living voice, embodies a conception or idea, the sayings of God, a decree, mandate or order; a continuous speaking discourse – instruction, doctrine, teaching, an account or reckoning, and the personal wisdom and power in union with God. For us to understand Logos, is for us to begin to know Elohyim – the triune God: Father, Son, and Holy Spirit.

He is living through the pages of scripture, the written accounts of God's heart toward His people. He is living in the declaration of God's spoken Word from eternity past through all eternity. He lives on through the personal wisdom and power that goes forth in union with God, the

Father and Holy Spirit. Logos has no beginning and no end! Today, I exhort you to partner with God - Logos, and speak forth life into this world and into your very being. As we come into agreement with the heart of God, His written Word, the very power of Logos embodies our decrees and releases God's purposes into the atmosphere. What an amazing thing it is to partner with Yahweh and see what He will do!

PRAYER: Father, today I ask that You show me how to partner with You in releasing Logos – the very spoken Word of God – Jesus Christ into every situation and circumstance. Help me to know You, not just as some distant God or words on a page, but the living breathing Logos. In Jesus' Name, Amen.

DAY 24

IMMANU EL
עממנואל

"GOD WITH US"

"Therefore the Lord Himself will give you a sign: Behold, the virgin shall conceive and bear a Son, and shall call His name Immanuel."
Isaiah 7:14

If we look closely enough, we can see images of Jesus in every book of the Bible. From Genesis to Revelation, the Messiah is. In the passage above, God shouts it from the mountain tops… "My Son is coming to the earth. Get ready!" We see a prophetic glimpse into the heart of God. He gives us the very name of His Son, and this name is no ordinary name.

Immanuel comes from the root word El meaning Elohiym (אלהים) – the Almighty One, and 'Im (עם) meaning with, unto, by, from between, and from among us. Not only did Immanuel come from man, but scripture tells us that He was the Word made flesh (John 1:14), and the only Begotten of the Father (John 3:16). In the name Immanuel, we see the God-man, Jesus.

It is exciting to see the pages of the Bible come alive as we study His Word, and begin to know the God of the universe. It is equally exciting to know that Immanuel, God with us is really with us! Yes, He walked the face of this planet, died, rose again, and ascended into heaven. If we stop there, we would think He has left us, but Jesus said it was good that He went away, because He would send Holy Spirit (John 16:7) – the third Person of the Trinity. We are not alone!

Today, be encouraged by Immanuel, our God who is with us. He sits at the right hand of the Father, making intercession for you (Hebrews 7:25), and Holy Spirit who is as close as your next breath. Need advice? Call out to Him and He'll answer you. Need comfort? Let Him to wrap you in His love. Allow the God of Creation (Genesis 1:1), Immanuel to uphold you and be with you today.

PRAYER: Father, thank You for always being with me. You came into the world in the form of man, so you could fully relate to humanity, and fully restore humanity. You came and You're still with me because of Your great love. I ask You to reveal Yourself to me today in unique ways that will always remind me that You are Immanuel, the God who is with me. In Jesus' Name, Amen.

DAY 25

HaMashiach Yeshua
משיח ישע

"Jesus the Messiah"

"...Concerning His Son Jesus Christ our Lord, who was born of the seed of David according to the flesh, and declared to be the Son of God with power according to the Spirit of holiness, by the resurrection from the dead." Romans 1:3- 4

In his book *Mere Christianity*, C.S. Lewis shares compelling evidence supporting HaMashiach Yeshua, Jesus the Messiah. He first asked this simple, yet powerful question, "Who do you say Jesus is?" These are familiar words as Jesus Himself asked this of His disciples, *"But who do you say that I am?" Simon Peter answered and said, "You are the Christ, the Son of the living God"* (Matthew 16:15-16). This is a question we must ask ourselves and others today.

Lewis went on to explain, *"I am trying here to prevent anyone saying the really foolish thing that people often say about Him: "I'm ready to accept Jesus as a great moral teacher, but I don't accept His claim to be God."*[3] At this, Lewis would share that a moral teacher would not make the claims Jesus made. If He were not God, then He was a liar or a lunatic.

From Genesis 1:1 to Revelation 22:21, we see HaMashiach Yeshua, Jesus the Messiah. He is neither liar nor lunatic, He is God. He is the image of the invisible God, the firstborn over all creation (Colossians 1:15). He is the Son of God and the Son of man. He is Mashiach ben Yosef – Messiah, son of Joseph. He was born of the Virgin Mary and raised by his earthly father Joseph. In His first coming, He is the suffering servant (Isaiah 53), who lived a sinless life and went to the cross, fulfilling prophecy in doing so. He is also Mashiach ben David – Messiah, son of David. In Revelation 22:16, He declared, *"I, Jesus, have sent My angel to testify to you these things in the churches. I am the Root and the Offspring of David, the Bright and Morning Star."* He is from the tribe of Judah, a descendant of David, and He will reign as King of Glory in His second coming.

If He was a liar, then humanity has fallen prey to the biggest deception of all time, and no one could call Him a "good moral teacher". If He was a lunatic, how was He able to live a life that fulfilled prophecies of old? And, where is the body? Scripture tells us that on the third day the stone was rolled away and the tomb where Jesus was buried was empty (John 20:1-10), that He ascended into heaven (Acts 1:9-11), and now sits at the right hand of God ever living to make intercession for us (Hebrews 7:25). If He is who He says He is, then He is HaMashiach Yeshua – Messiah – Jesus, the Christ! He is the second Adam who has redeemed mankind (I Corinthians 15:45), and He is the coming King of kings who will reign for all eternity (Revelation 22:7). Who do you say He is?

PRAYER: Father, thank You for sending Your only Son Jesus. He is the Word in the flesh, the express image of You – He is God and He is Messiah. Where I have wrong views of Jesus, I ask You to correct them. Help me to fully know HaMashiach Yeshua. In Jesus' Name, Amen.

DAY 26

CHATAN
חתן

"BRIDEGROOM"

"For as a young man marries a virgin, so shall your sons marry you; and as the bridegroom rejoices over the bride, so shall your God rejoice over you." Isaiah 62:5

"He who has the bride is the bridegroom; but the friend of the bridegroom, who stands and hears him, rejoices greatly because of the bridegroom's voice. Therefore this joy of mine is fulfilled." John 3:29

There is something so beautiful and magical in that moment when a bridegroom sees his bride for the first time as she walks down the aisle on their wedding day. The corners of his mouth begin to turn upward into a beaming smile, his eyes sparkle – this is a man in love and you can see it all over him. That moment is as perfect as things can be this side of eternity. Then, their eyes meet in that moment and time seems to stand still. In that moment love and joy collide. This is a sacred moment!

"...so shall your God rejoice over you," says Isaiah. Our God is the Bridegroom of the ages who rejoices over His bride, the church, the body of Christ, you! Chatan, our Bridegroom desires intimate knowledge of His people. His heart is overwhelmed with every ounce of love He has

when your eyes meet His. He longs for His beloved ones to gaze upon Him and to know His heart.

King David understood his place as a bride in the Kingdom of Heaven. In Psalm 27:4, he says, *"One thing I have desired of the LORD, that will I seek: That I may dwell in the house of the LORD all the days of my life, to behold the beauty of the LORD, and to inquire in His temple."* David's one desire was to gaze into the eyes of pure beauty, his Chatan; and see delight reflecting back at him. Have you seen His delight?

John the Baptist spoke as being the friend of Bridegroom in the passage above. He describes the wedding from a slightly different vantage point. He explains what the groomsmen hear. There is something noticeable in the Bridegroom's voice. It is the sound of love, the sound of the rejoicing heart. Have you heard His voice rejoice over you?

Jesus, our Bridegroom eagerly waits for the wedding of the ages – the day when His Father opens the door for the Bride to enter. On that day, the culmination of all time, He will gaze lovingly into His beloved's eyes and receive her as His own.

Today, hear Him say to you, *"I will betroth you to Me forever; Yes, I will betroth you to Me in righteousness and justice, in loving-kindness and mercy; I will betroth you to Me in faithfulness, and you shall know the LORD"* (Hosea 2:19-20). Chatan, our Bridegroom is waiting for you to draw near to Him, to gaze into His eyes of love, to hear His song of love, and know His delight. Today He invites you to be His bride!

ᏢRAYER: Father, my heart cannot even begin to understand the love You have for me as the Bridegroom, Chatan. Thank you for making a way for me to be Your bride, the desire of Your heart, the object of Your affections. I ask You to show me Your heart as I gaze upon Your beauty and see into Your eyes. In Jesus' Name, Amen.

DAY 27

RUACH ADONAI
רוח אדון

"THE SPIRIT OF THE LORD"

"The Spirit of the LORD shall rest upon Him, the Spirit of wisdom and understanding, the Spirit of counsel and might, the Spirit of knowledge and of the fear of the LORD." Isaiah 11:2

We cannot see wind, yet we can feel it. On a warm spring day, there is nothing more comforting and peaceful than the warm wind gently rushing through the trees. We cannot see the wind, but we can see its affects on our surrounding. During a storm, this wind can destroy buildings. We cannot see the wind; however, we know its power. When harnessed, wind can power many things. We cannot see the wind, but there is no doubt of its existence.

In a like manner, we cannot see Ruach Adonai, the Spirit of the Lord, yet there is no doubt this third person of the Trinity is real. Many of us do not really know Holy Spirit though. We reference the Spirit as some object – an "it". However, He is very much a person, no less God than the Father or Jesus, the Son. He is coequal in power and coeternal. He is Elohiym from Genesis 1:1, the power, breath, and mind of God. He is one with God the Father and Son, but manifests Himself in various ways.

Isaiah gives us a small glimpse into the character of Ruach Adonai in today's scripture. He is the Spirit of the Lord, who expresses Himself as

Wisdom, Understanding, Counsel, Might, Knowledge, and Awe or Fear we have for the Lord. He leads us into truth, because He is the Spirit of Truth (John 16:13). He is the One who came into the Upper Room on Pentecost, empowering the 120 who were there (Acts 2). He dwells within the believer, drawing them closer to the Father and Jesus (John 14:16-17).

Is there a place in your life where you need greater understanding and wisdom? Call upon Ruach Adonai to open the eyes of your understanding – He is Wisdom and Revelation (Ephesians 1:17-18). Do you need strength to walk out a situation? The Spirit of the Lord will give you counsel and might. He is your Helper. He is the very breath and wind of God. Permit Ruach Adanai to breathe peace, and blow the sweet winds of Heaven upon you, creating awe in your spirit, as He draws you into the presence and heart of God.

PRAYER: Father, I love You. You are such a multi-faceted God. The more I come to know You, the more I realize I really don't know You very well at all. Ruach Adonai, You are God. You are not a thing. Help me to know You more. I want to be Your friend. Walk and talk with me today – lead me into the knowledge of God. In Jesus' Name, Amen.

DAY 28

EL EMET
אל אמת

"THE GOD OF TRUTH"

"Into Your hand I commit my spirit; You have redeemed me,
O LORD God of truth." Psalm 31:5

In today's passage, the psalmist makes a very powerful declaration – I commit my life to You, God. I trust You with all things, because you have redeemed and saved me from my enemies. I have known You as El Emet, the God of Truth. You are firm, faithful, reliable, and sure. Time and time again, You have given divine instruction – instruction that has saved my soul. The psalmist knew without a doubt who his God was!

Have you ever heard the phrase, "If God said it that settles it?" What if God's words are contrary to what are facts in the natural? Do you know El Emet, the God of Truth? In our lives we will face enemies just like the psalmist. Our enemies may not be a foreign people attempting to take our land, but they are as real as the enemies in biblical times. Perhaps your enemy is economic and your bank balance is dismal. God says He is your provider (Genesis 22). Maybe sickness and disease are what you're battling and the physician has given you little hope. El Emet says His desire if for you to prosper and be in health, even as your soul prospers (III John 1:2). No matter what the earthly facts may say, the Word of Truth from El Emet is the final word. He is not a man that He should lie

(Numbers 23:19) – He is truth! Do you trust Him enough to commit your life to His keeping?

PRAYER: Father, I admit there are times I believe the report from man more than I trust Your Word. In my journey to knowing You, I ask You to pour out a Spirit of Wisdom and Revelation. Reveal Yourself to me as El Emet, the God of Truth, and help me to believe You no matter what things look like in the natural. In Jesus' Name, Amen.

DAY 29

EL SHADDAI
אל שדדי

"GOD ALMIGHTY...
THE ALL-SUFFICIENT GOD"

"When Abram was ninety-nine years old, the LORD appeared to Abram and said to him, "I am Almighty God; walk before Me and be blameless. And I will make My covenant between Me and you, and will multiply you exceedingly..." Genesis 17:1-2

"May God Almighty bless you, and make you fruitful and multiply you, that you may be an assembly of peoples..." Genesis 28:3

"Also God said to him: 'I am God Almighty. Be fruitful and multiply; a nation and a company of nations shall proceed from you, and kings shall come from your body.'" Genesis 35:11

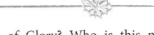

Who is this King of Glory? Who is this mighty God, whose voice thunders? Who is this Father, strong and firm; unmovable? He is El Shaddai, the almighty God, who is also the All-Sufficient God.

There is debate as to the true meaning of El Shaddai. Many English translations suggest the word is derived from the root *Shadad*, which means to overpower. However, *Shad* is Hebrew for "breast". Indeed, our

Father God is a mighty warrior, the One who fights the battles for us - but equal to His strength and father heart is the tender mother heart of God. This is not a question of gender, but a revelation of His character.

So many refuse to understand this facet of God: Father, Son and Holy Spirit, but it is the tenderness of God that longs for a people to commune with, to once again fellowship with as He did daily with Adam before the fall. He yearns to gather His people and protect them like a hen gathers her chicks under her wings (Matthew 23:37). He rejoices over His children, as we lean upon Him for comfort and peace. Like a mother feeding and rocking her infant child, the tender-hearted One holds us, kisses the bruises, warms us with a smile, watches over us, and gives us the pure milk of His Word (1 Peter 2:2).

This characteristic of God by no means makes Him weak or over emotional. Yet, our God, El Shaddai, the many breasted and all sufficient One is full of longing, affection, and pure emotion. As endless as His might and power are, so is His tenderness, gentleness, and mercy. Today, rest under the shadow of the Almighty's wings (Psalm 91) and allow Him to reveal His nurturing heart; a heart that desires to bless You and see your life be fruitful.

PRAYER: Father, I am in awe of how great You are. It is difficult at times to fathom such a multi-faceted God. Just when I think I am beginning to understand who You are, You reveal yet another aspect of Your character. Today, reveal to me the tender-hearted nurturer, and the One who desires to see my life be fruitful. Help me to understand Your strength and Your sensitivity – the kindhearted affectionate Lord Almighty. In Jesus' Name, Amen.

DAY 30

PARAKLETOS
Παράκλητος

"THE COMFORTER"

*"But the Helper, the Holy Spirit, whom the Father will send in
My name, He will teach you all things, and bring to your
remembrance all things that I said to you." John 14:26*

Just when things seemed to be going so well, Jesus sat down with His
disciples and told them of His impending death. Even though they had
walked with Him for three years, they still thought He was going to
overthrow the government of the time and become the King, but Jesus
was speaking of a Heavenly Kingdom. These twelve young men were
freaking out with the thought of Jesus leaving them. What would they do
without their Rabbi? Who would lead them in the Way? In the midst of
their uneasiness, Jesus assured them He would not leave them alone, but
would send the Comforter - Parakletos – Holy Spirit.

When Jesus left the earth to sit at the Father's right hand, He sent
Parakletos, One who did not simply come in His stead, but One who was
just like Him. Jesus sent the Advocate - a counselor who pleads our case
and defends us; the Helper – someone to come alongside and give aid
and guidance; the Comforter – the very Breathe of God (Pneuma), who
empowers us to walk out this life in Christ, here on the earth. Parakletos,
the third Person of the Trinity, also keeps us in remembrance of the

Father, and Jesus. He leads us into all truth, because He is Truth – He is God!

We have a great promise from God in Hebrews 13:5. He says, *"Never will I leave or forsake you."* Jesus assured us that He would be with us always (Matthew 28:20), and He fulfilled this promise when the Comforter, Parakletos came. Are you feeling uneasy with the life you're currently living? Do you need someone to help you remember who you are in Christ? We may not have Jesus in the flesh walking with us like the disciples did, but Parakletos is no understudy. He is the One who is with us in all circumstances, and He desires to be our closest friend. Today, ask the Comforter to surround you with His presence, drawing you closer to the heart of God.

PRAYER: Father, so often we consider Holy Spirit to be somewhat less than God, but He is co-equal to You and Jesus. Thank You for sending the Comforter, the Helper, our Advocate – Parakletos. I pray that You, Holy Spirit will lead me and guide me into truth. Help me to know You better, as I long to know God. In Jesus' Name, Amen.

DAY 31

EL OLAM
אל עולם

"THE EVERLASTING GOD"

*"Have you not known? Have you not heard? The everlasting God,
the LORD, the Creator of the ends of the earth, neither faints nor is
weary. His understanding is unsearchable. He gives power to the
weak, and to those who have no might He increases strength. Even
the youths shall faint and be weary, and the young men shall utterly
fall, but those who wait on the LORD shall renew their strength; they
shall mount up with wings like eagles, they shall run and not be
weary, they shall walk and not faint." Isaiah 40:28-31*

There is absolutely nothing more comforting and at the same time more
exhilarating than to know we serve an eternal God. Elohiym; our God
from Genesis 1:1, who opened the door to the greatest mystery of life
itself – His character is also El Olam, the everlasting God. Have you
heard Him speaking to you as you have studied His Names? Do you
know the One who created the universe by His word and holds time itself
in the palm of His hands? He is the Ancient of Days; the One who was,
who is, and who always will be. His future is unending and His reach is
eternal. He is our forever God.

The root word for Olam is 'Alam (עלם), which means to conceal or to
hide. Proverbs 25:2 says, *"It is the glory of God to conceal a matter, but the
glory of kings is to search out a matter."* The invitation is sitting before

133

you. El Olam desires for you to search Him out, to tangle yourself up in Him, and weave your life into the tapestry of the ages. Will you wait upon the Lord today, tomorrow; in times of struggle or peace? For the willing, we have a beautiful promise. He offers to exchange our weakness for His power; our weariness for His strength; our limits for His unlimited eternal life.

Let today be the beginning of your eternal journey of knowing the heart of God. Allow El Olam, the Everlasting God to lift you up on His wings. Soar in His peace, mercy, grace, and eternal love!

PRAYER: Father, You are the Source of life and I love You so much. There are no words that accurately convey the gratitude and awe I have in my heart for You. Give me strength to continue this journey of searching the Unsearchable One. I want to finish the race and hear You say, "Well done!"

AFTERWORDS

While writing this book, I had moments of intense joy, moments of sobering realization, and moments of amazing new revelation. I found myself surrounded by God and at times, overcome by His presence. I was overwhelmed by His goodness and love, as He and I crafted these pages. He loves to partner with His children!

It is my earnest prayer that these last 31 days have brought similar moments for you, as you've come to know God through His names. A name is a powerful thing and reveals much about a person and their character. Isn't it odd how we seem to *fit our names*? All of who God is has been encapsulated in His names. Names He chose to reveal to His people.

Allow this to be a starting point, an introduction for you in knowing God intimately. There are volumes yet to be written of His character, goodness, and love. Perhaps as you continue to study, He will partner with you to make known the deeper things of His heart!

"The LORD bless you and keep you;
the LORD make His face shine upon you, and be gracious to you;
the LORD lift up His countenance upon you, and give you peace."
Numbers 6:24-26

Yivarechicha Adonai V'yishmirecha;
Ya-Ayr Adonai panav Aylecha v'yichunecha;
Yee-saw Adonai panav Aylecha v'ya-saym l'cha shalom.

May Yahweh bless you in your pursuit to know Him.

In Christ's Love,
Connie V. Scott

END NOTES

Throughout the writing of this book, I used the following sources for information and inspiration. I hope these resources will be helpful to you as you continue your studies.

1. Emaar pjsc. (2009). *Burj Khalifa*. Retrieved on March 25, 2011 from http://www.burjkhalifa.ae/language/en-us/home.aspx

2. Mote, Edward. (1834). *The Solid Rock*. Copyright: Public Domain

3. Lewis, C.S. (2001). *Mere Christianity*. Harper, San Francisco, CA.

APPENDIX

To aid you in your studies of the Names of God contained in this book, we have provided the phonetic pronunciation for each day.

∾ **Day 1: Elohiym** [ehl-oh-HEEM] – The Almighty One

∾ **Day 2: Elohay Kedem** [ehl-O-hay ked-Dem] – God of the Beginning

∾ **Day 3: Abba** [ab-bah'] – Father

∾ **Day 4: Elohay Kedoshim** [ehl-O-hay Keh-dOsh-eem] / **El HaKadosh** [ehl Ha-Kah-dOsh] – The Holy God

∾ **Day 5: YHVH M'Kadesh** [M'Ka-dey-sh] – The Lord Who Makes Holy

∾ **Day 6: YHVH** [yeh-ho-vaw' / ah-doh-NIE / yah-vvehy] – LORD

∾ **Day 7: Elohiym Chaiyim** [ehl-oh-HEEM khah'-ee-Eem] – The Living God

∾ **Day 8: El Elyon** [ehl elyown] – The Most High God

∾ **Day 9: YHVH Kanna** [Kan-nah] – The Jealous God

∾ **Day 10: Esh Okhlah** [ehsh-O-ka-lah] – Consuming Fire

∾ **Day 11: Elohay Tehilati** [ehl-O-hay teh-Hee-la-Tee] – God of My Praise

∾ **Day 12: El Ro'i** [ehl rO-ee] – The God Who Sees

∾ **Day 13: YHVH Yir'eh** [Year-eh] – The Lord Who Sees and Provides

∾ **Day 14: El HaNe'eman** [ehl Ha-Neh-eh-man] – The Faithful God

∾ **Day 15: YHVH Shalom** [sha-lohm] The LORD is Peace

- **Day 16: Adonai Tzuri** [ah-doh-NIE tzoo-ree] – God of My Strength/God My Rock

- **Day 17: Jehovah Rohi** [yeh-ho-vaw Ro-eh] – The Lord My Shepherd

- **Day 18: Jehovah Roph'ekha** [yeh-ho-vaw ropha-ekcha] – The Lord Heals

- **Day 19: Jehovah Nissi** [yeh-ho-vaw nee-cee] – The Lord My Banner

- **Day 20: Adonai** [ah-doh-NIE] – LORD

- **Day 21: Elohay Mishpat** [ehl-O-hay meesh-pot] – God of Justice

- **Day 22: El Yeshuati** [ehl Yish-oo-Ah-tee] – The God of My Salvation

- **Day 23: Logos** [log'-os] – The Word

- **Day 24: Immanu El** [Ee-Man-OO-ehl] – God with Us

- **Day 25: HaMashiach Yeshua** [Ha-Mah-Shee-ahwk yeh-shoo-Ah] – Jesus the Messiah

- **Day 26: Chatan** [khaw-thawn'] – Bridegroom

- **Day 27: Ruach Adonai** [Roo-awk ah-doh-NIE] – The Spirit of the Lord

- **Day 28: El Emet** [ehl em-et] – The God of Truth

- **Day 29: El Shaddai** [Ehl shad-dah'-ee] – God Almighty/ The All-Sufficient God

- **Day 30: Parakletos** [par-ak'-lay-tos] – The Comforter

- **Day 31: El OLAM** [ehl oh-lam] – The Everlasting God

GOD'S PLAN

We Have All Sinned
"For all have sinned and fall short of the glory of God." Romans 3:23

The Penalty for Sin is Death
"The wages of sin is death, but the gift of God is eternal life through Jesus Christ our Lord. Romans 6:23

God Provides a Way
"God demonstrates His own love for us, in that while we were yet sinners Christ died for us." Romans 5:8

Prayer to Receive Jesus, as Savior and Lord

Father, I come to You in the Name of Jesus. Your Word says in Romans 10:13, "All who call upon the Name of the Lord will be saved." I believe Your Word to be true, so I know You hear my prayers and will bring me into Salvation.

Lord, I understand I am a sinner in need of a Savior. I believe You sent Your one and only Son, Jesus into the world to save humanity. Jesus, You lived a sinless life, yet humbly gave it all for me. I believe you died on the cross, were buried in a grave, and rose again on the third day. I believe You are the Son of God, and the Savior of the world.

Jesus, I ask You to come into my life - be my Savior, my Master, and my Friend. Forgive me of all my sin and make me clean in the sight of God. I believe in my heart and confess with my mouth, "You are Lord of my life and heaven is my eternal destination, because my name is written in the Book of Life. Through the power of Holy Spirit, I can and will live a life that is pleasing to You." Thank You for this new life. In Jesus' Name, Amen.

THE NEXT STEP

If you just prayed the prayer on the previous page, I want to personally congratulate you and say, "Welcome to the family of God!" There is no greater decision in life than to choose to follow the risen Lord Jesus. This is just the beginning of your new life in God. Below are a few things I think will help you along the way. God bless You! - Connie

- ❧ **Tell someone you have accepted Jesus, as Lord and Savior.** The Bible tells us in Romans 10:10, *"For with the heart one believes unto righteousness and with the mouth confession is made unto salvation."* Allow someone to share the joy of your salvation with you.

- ❧ **Purchase a good study Bible and begin to read it everyday.** Don't worry about what *version* it is; just choose one that you can clearly understand. I suggest you begin reading about God's love for you in the Book of John.

- ❧ **Pray to God everyday.** Prayer is not some mystical thing we do as Christians. It is simply talking to God. Be as real with Him, as you would with your best friend. Make prayer your first priority of the day. If you begin and end your day with Him, everything in between works out much better.

- ❧ **Find a good Bible believing church and attend regularly.** Church is not a man idea, but a God idea (Hebrews 10:24-25)! We attend church to be taught the Word of God, to worship Him with other believers, and to connect with a community of people who share our faith.

- ❧ **Community is important.** God does not expect us to do it all alone. Begin to spend time with other believers. There is nothing like a good Christian friend to share your challenges and triumphs with!

ABOUT THE AUTHOR

Rev. Connie V. Scott

In 1985, some friends invited Connie to join their church choir. Little did she know that God was setting her up! A year later, in June of 1986, Connie accepted Jesus as her Lord and Savior. Her love for music didn't change, but her focus did. Instead of seeking glory, she was giving it to God. Connie continued singing with church choirs and worship teams, while attending Central Wyoming College on a Vocal Music scholarship. After earning her A.A. degree in music, Connie returned to Evanston, Wyoming, to worship at Crossroads Newlife Fellowship. In 1994, she became the Worship Pastor at CNF and served in that position until December 2005.

With a huge desire to share her love for biblical worship and Christian music, Connie founded Voice of Hope Ministries, in 2001. That same year, she became an ordained minister. It was at this time God began speaking to Connie about writing books. Placing *book writing* on the shelf, Connie, and some friends formed the vocal group Pearl. Pearl released a CD in 2003, which Connie co-wrote and sang several songs.

Feeling a redirect from God, Connie stepped out on her own in 2004, to minister through the various outreaches of Voice of Hope Ministries. Now was the time to begin the journey of writing a book, or in this case, one of many to come!

Connie is an itinerant speaker, songwriter, recording artist, author, and seasoned worship leader. Her teaching and vocal styles are unique and varied, which allow her to impact the lives of many people. Connie's vision, as well as that of Voice of Hope Ministries is simple: Exalt the Name of Jesus and see the Body of Christ become a people of worship!

VOICE OF HOPE MINISTRIES

"Write the vision and make it plain..." (Habakkuk 2:2). While still attending college, God spoke "the vision" of Voice of Hope Ministries to Connie's heart. In 2001, after much prayer and preparation, she took those first steps in seeing that vision come to pass. VOH launched its first website and Connie began to do concerts and ministry events.

In 2004, VOH became a non-profit corporation. Today, VOH is a non-profit, tax-exempt (501c3) corporation, seeking to minister wherever God leads. Currently, VOH has several outreach ministries, serving and ministering to people throughout the Inner Mountain West. Our goal is to build this ministry by adding various outreaches that will continue to fulfill the vision – *Keeping hope alive by touching lives through Worship and the Word of God!*

At Voice of Hope Ministries,
We seek to:

- Touch lives through Worship and the Word!

- Minister Christ's love and salvation through original music and biblical teaching.

- Strengthen and encourage the body of Christ in their faith through songs and teachings.

- Teach on biblical worship and how it pertains to the believer's life.

- Work with local Christian churches & organizations to minister the Gospel of Jesus Christ to all who are willing to hear.

- Train and equip the church on practical elements of worship ministry.

For more information regarding Voice of Hope Ministries, please contact our office at: PO Box 2344, Evanston, WY 82930, call (307) 679-2616 or visit our website – www.vohministries.org.

PRODUCTS

Check out these other products from
Voice of Hope Ministries

"Seasons Change"
- Connie V. Scott

This is Connie's solo recording project, released January 2006. Seasons Change will take you on a journey into the presence of God. No matter what your life situation, you will relate to Connie's honest and heartfelt writing. *Price: $15.00 each*

"I Will Seek Your Face:
31 Days of Worship & Praise"
- Rev. Connie V. Scott

Released in the fall of 2005, "Worship & Praise" is the first book in this devotional series, written by Connie Scott. Spend 31 days growing in intimacy with God. Intimacy does not begin in the church service, but in the privates times we spend with the Lord. *Price: $10.00 each*

"Knowing You"
- Pearl

Released in 2003, this is Connie's first CD with the vocal group Pearl. Blending strong vocals with exceptional instrumentation, Pearl's debut CD is sure to bless people from all age groups and musical tastes. *Price: $10.00 each*

Teaching CD's by Connie Scott

Connie has a number of teachings available to deepen your walk with the Lord, and challenge you as you press in to know God more. Below is a list of available teachings. *Price: $7.00 each (singles) / $12.00 each (double) / $15.00 each (mp3) / $25.00 each (conference teachings)*

- ∾ *Anointings, Encounters, or Intimacy*
- ∾ *Are You Expecting... What?*
- ∾ *Don't Miss the Hour of Your Visitation*
- ∾ *Getting Practical*
- ∾ *Oil of Intimacy*
- ∾ *Rebuilding the Foundation*
- ∾ *Step it Up*
- ∾ *Walking in the Outpouring of the Promise*
- ∾ *The Praise Series (2 Disk Teaching)*
- ∾ *Great Expectations Conference (MP3 or CD)*

Worship Junkie ᵀᴹ Products

Created by Connie Scott and Wendy Jepsen, "Worship Junkie"™ has become a serious expression of the very passion of their hearts. Psalm 27:4 says, *"One thing I desire of the Lord, this I will seek, that I may dwell in the house of the Lord all the days of my life, to behold the beauty of the Lord, and to inquire in His temple."*

A junkie is someone who has an unquenchable appetite for something. In this case, we are *worship junkies* wishing to express this unquenchable desire we have for the Bridegroom King, Jesus! He is the One we long to know more every day and will worship for all eternity. We proudly wear our designs and hope you'll be bold enough to tell others that you are a "Worship Junkie"™ too!

To purchase more copies of this book or other products by Connie Scott contact Voice of Hope Ministries at (307) 679-2616 or visit our web site at:
http://www.vohministries.org

Made in the USA
Charleston, SC
24 June 2013